before we marry

Written &
Illustrated
by
Adilah Eleam

A communicator journal for couples considering marriage.

"Before We Marry"

Communicator Journal/Keepsake

This book is intended for personal reflection and communication purposes only. It is not a substitute for professional counseling, legal advice, or therapy. The author and publisher disclaim any liability arising directly or indirectly from the use of this book.

Cover Design by: Adilah Eleam
Published by: Jacinth Media Productions
Info@JacinthMediaProductions
Allentown, Pennsylvania
ISBN 978-1-960594-34-1
LCCN# 2025941254

First Edition

For permissions, inquiries, or more information, please contact:
Addieeleam@gmail.com

i

This book is dedicated to...
YOUR SERENITY

"Before We Marry"
Communicator Journal/Keepsake

WELCOME

THIS JOURNAL IS FOR COUPLES GETTING READY TO SAY "I DO"—BUT WANT TO START STRONG, TOGETHER.

INSIDE, YOU'LL FIND THOUGHTFUL QUESTIONS AND FUN PROMPTS TO HELP YOU TALK ABOUT REAL-LIFE THINGS: LOVE, VALUES, MONEY, FAMILY, DAILY LIFE, AND MORE.

IT'S NOT ABOUT BEING PERFECT—IT'S ABOUT BEING HONEST, OPEN, AND READY TO BUILD A HEALTHY, HAPPY FUTURE.

TAKE YOUR TIME. HAVE THE DEEP TALKS. LAUGH A LITTLE. LEARN A LOT.

THIS IS YOUR SPACE TO GROW CLOSER—BEFORE YOU GROW OLD TOGETHER.

"Before We Marry"

Communicator Journal/Keepsake

How to Use This Journal
For couples thinking about marriage

Thinking about getting married? This journal is here to help you talk, laugh, and get real with each other before you say "I do."

Here's how to use it:

Take your time. Go through the pages at your own pace—no rush.

Be honest. Say what's real for you, even if it's not perfect.

Work together. Some pages are for talking, some are for writing —do what feels right.

Keep it kind. Listen without judgement. Be open, not defensive.

Make it fun. Marriage is serious, but this doesn't have to be heavy all the time.

Use this journal to connect, reflect, and see where you're both at. It's not about having all the answers—it's about starting the right conversations.

Let's begin.

 **Introduction**

Marriage is a grand adventure, a loving partnership where you grow together and share a lifetime commitment. Preparing for your wedding day's details is important, but equally important is preparing for the lifelong commitment ahead. This book helps you have the necessary conversations, share meaningful experiences and engage in personal reflections to strengthen your relationship before saying "I do."

It offers several prompts for deep discussions, many connection-building activities and ample space to record your shared thoughts and memories. This keepsake will serve as an important reminder of your origins, whether you're pursuing shared aspirations, facing difficulties, or simply enjoying your romance.

This journal promotes open communication, shared laughter and a strong, fulfilling marriage. Successful marriages aren't accidental; they're built on intentional work, understanding each other and meaningful love.

Your Picture Here

Our Story

This love story belongs to

&

vi

Table of Contents

*Extra blank sheets in back of book.

"Before We Marry"
Communicator Journal/Keepsake

Part 1
"Us"

Our Love Story...

How We Met

_____

_____

_____

_____

_____

_____

_____

_____

_____

Our Favorite Memories Together

"Before We Marry"

Communicator Journal/Keepsake

Part 2

"What Marriage means to Us"

What Marriage Means to Us

♥ ♥ ♥

What does a healthy marriage look like to us?

_____

_____

_____

_____

_____

_____

_____

_____

_____

_____

_____

_____

_____

_____

_____

_____

_____

What Marriage Means to Us Continued...

_____

_____

_____

_____

_____

_____

_____

_____

_____

_____

_____

_____

_____

_____

_____

Why We Want To Get Married?

_____

_____

_____

_____

_____

_____

_____

_____

_____

_____

_____

_____

_____

_____

Why We Want To Get Married?
Continued...

_____

_____

_____

_____

_____

_____

_____

_____

_____

_____

_____

_____

_____

_____

OUR HOPES AND DREAMS...

What are our hopes and dreams for our marriage?

_____

_____

_____

_____

_____

_____

_____

_____

_____

_____

_____

_____

_____

_____

HOPE is a waking dream

OUR HOPES AND DREAMS CONTINUED...

_____

_____

_____

_____

_____

_____

_____

_____

_____

_____

_____

"Before We Marry"

Communicator Journal/Keepsake

Part 3

"Communication & Conflict"

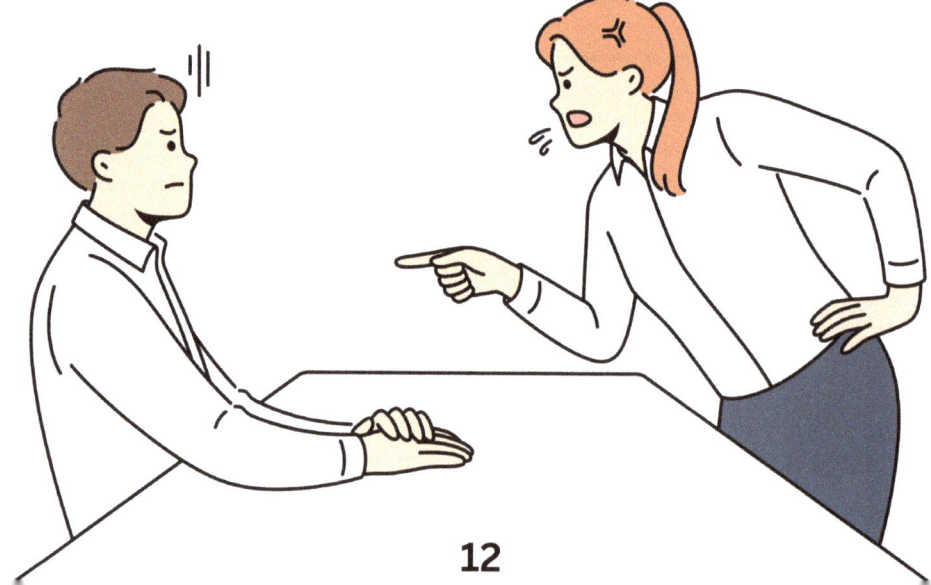

How We Express Love & Appreciation

Share some ways you show love and appreciation to your partner?

How We Handle Disagreements

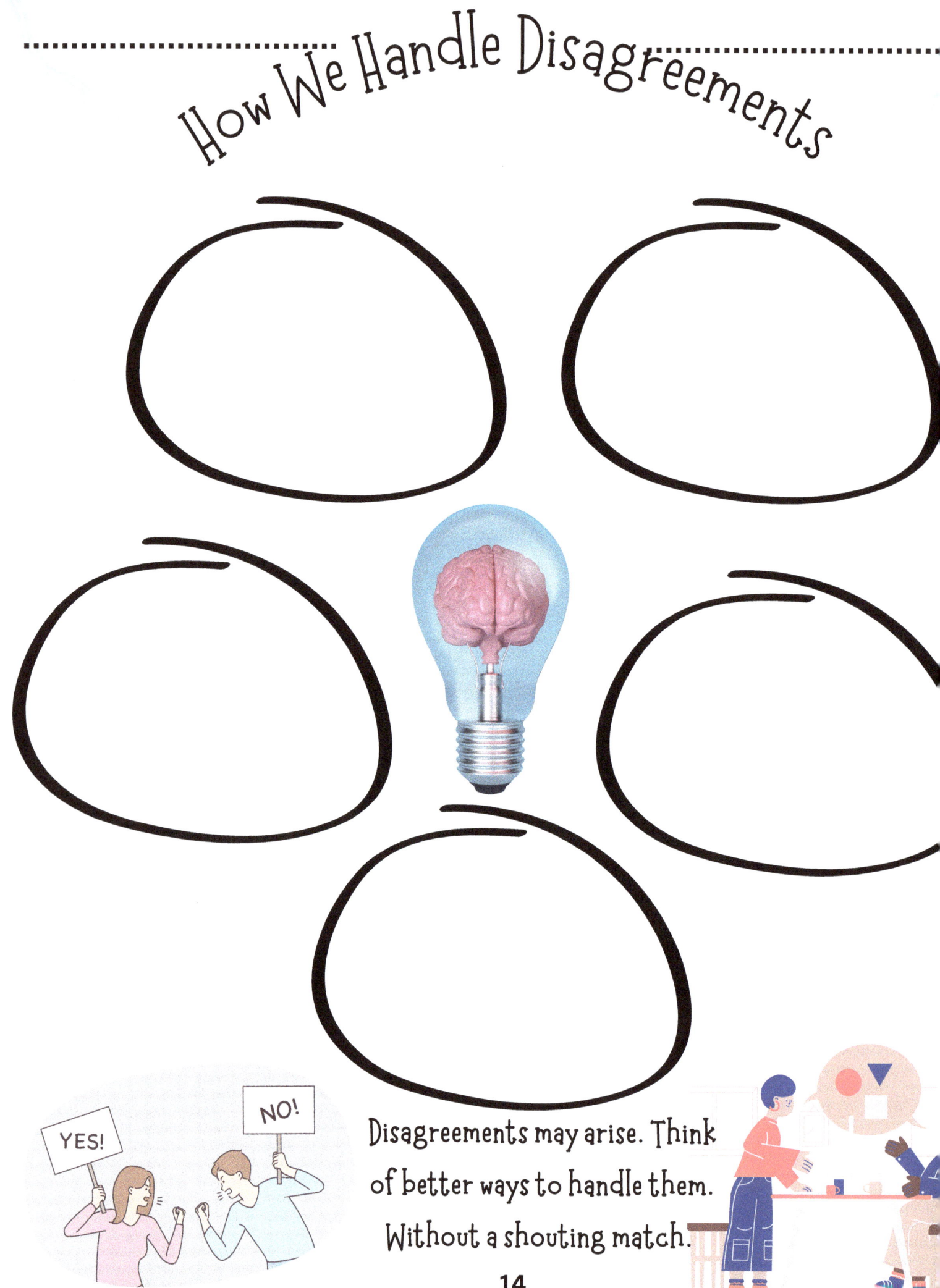

Disagreements may arise. Think of better ways to handle them. Without a shouting match.

YES!

NO!

OUR CONFLICT RESOLUTION STRATEGIES

Fill in different strategies to peacefully and respectfully settle conflicts. (As much as possible)

"Before We Marry"

Communicator Journal/Keepsake

Part 4

"Family & Background"

How Our Upbringings Influence Our Views on Marriage

HOW DO WE SEE MARRIAGE BASED ON HOW WE GREW UP? GOOD OR BAD LET'S TALK ABOUT IT!

Traditions We Want to Continue or Create

What traditions would you like to continue?

What traditions would you like to start together?

_____
_____
_____
_____
_____
_____
_____
_____
_____
_____
_____
_____
_____
_____
_____
_____
_____
_____

_____
_____
_____
_____
_____
_____
_____
_____
_____
_____
_____
_____
_____
_____
_____
_____

How We Plan to Navigate Family Dynamics

Use this page to talk about how you'll handle family stuff together. Think about boundaries, traditions, visits, and anything else that matters.

_____
_____
_____
_____
_____
_____
_____
_____
_____
_____
_____
_____
_____
_____
_____
_____
_____
_____
_____
_____
_____
_____
_____
_____

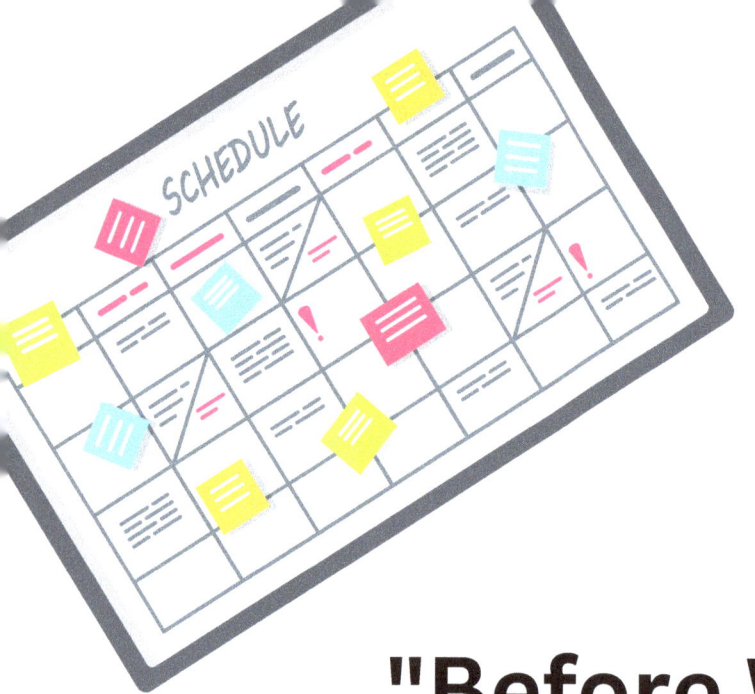

"Before We Marry"

Communicator Journal/Keepsake

Part 5

"Goals & Future Planning"

OUR INDIVIDUAL & SHARED LIFE GOALS

What are some goals you have for yourself, individually and together?

CHASE goals

Yours, Mine & Ours

Next level

goals

Career Aspirations and Work-Life Balance

**What are are your career Aspirations? How do you plan
to balance work and home life?**

Where We See Ourselves in 5 years

Talk about things like life, careers and where you might live.

_____

_____

_____

_____

_____

_____

_____

_____

_____

_____

_____

_____

_____

_____

Talk about things like life, careers and where you might live.

WHERE WE SEE OURSELVES IN 10 YEARS?

Where We See Ourselves in 20 years?

"Before We Marry"

Communicator Journal/Keepsake

Part 6

"Love Languages & Personality"

Love Language Quiz Included

You are doing great ☺

Love Language Quiz

Pick the answers that best describe you.

1. When I'm feeling down, I feel most loved when:

A) Someone gives me a thoughtful gift.

B) Someone spends quality time with me, even if we're doing nothing.

C) Someone expresses their love for me through words.

D) Someone gives me a hug or holds my hand.

E) Someone does something for me to lighten my load (e.g., helps with chores).

2. I feel closest to my partner when:

A) We share meaningful gifts with each other.

B) We engage in deep conversations.

C) We spend time doing activities together.

D) We show physical affection.

E) We do things for each other without being asked.

3. If I were given the option to receive a gift or a heartfelt note, I would prefer:

A) A heartfelt note with personal words.

B) A thoughtful gift that shows effort.

C) A spontaneous hug or kiss.

D) Spending quality time together.

E) Someone helping me with something I've been struggling with.

Love Language Quiz Continued...

4. When I'm upset, I feel better when:

A) Someone listens to me without judgment and talks things through.

B) I'm given personal space, but we later talk things through.

C) Someone does something special for me.

D) Someone touches or comforts me physically.

E) Someone helps me with my responsibilities or tasks.

5. To show someone I care, I often:

A) Give them thoughtful gifts.

B) Write them a heartfelt message or speak affirming words.

C) Spend time with them, sharing experiences.

D) Offer physical affection, like hugs or holding hands.

E) Lend a hand with something they need help with.

Scoring:

Mostly **A's**: Your love language is **Receiving Gifts**

Mostly **B's**: Your love language is **Words of Affirmation**

Mostly **C's**: Your love language is **Quality Time**

Mostly **D's**: Your love language is **Physical Touch**

Mostly **E's**: Your love language is **Acts of Service**

Our Love Languages

**Talk About How Your Love Languages
Speak to each Other
Or
The Similarities and/or Differences.**

Personality Traits and How They Complement Each Other

Check personality traits in back of book.

_____

_____

_____

_____

_____

_____

_____

_____

_____

_____

_____

_____

_____

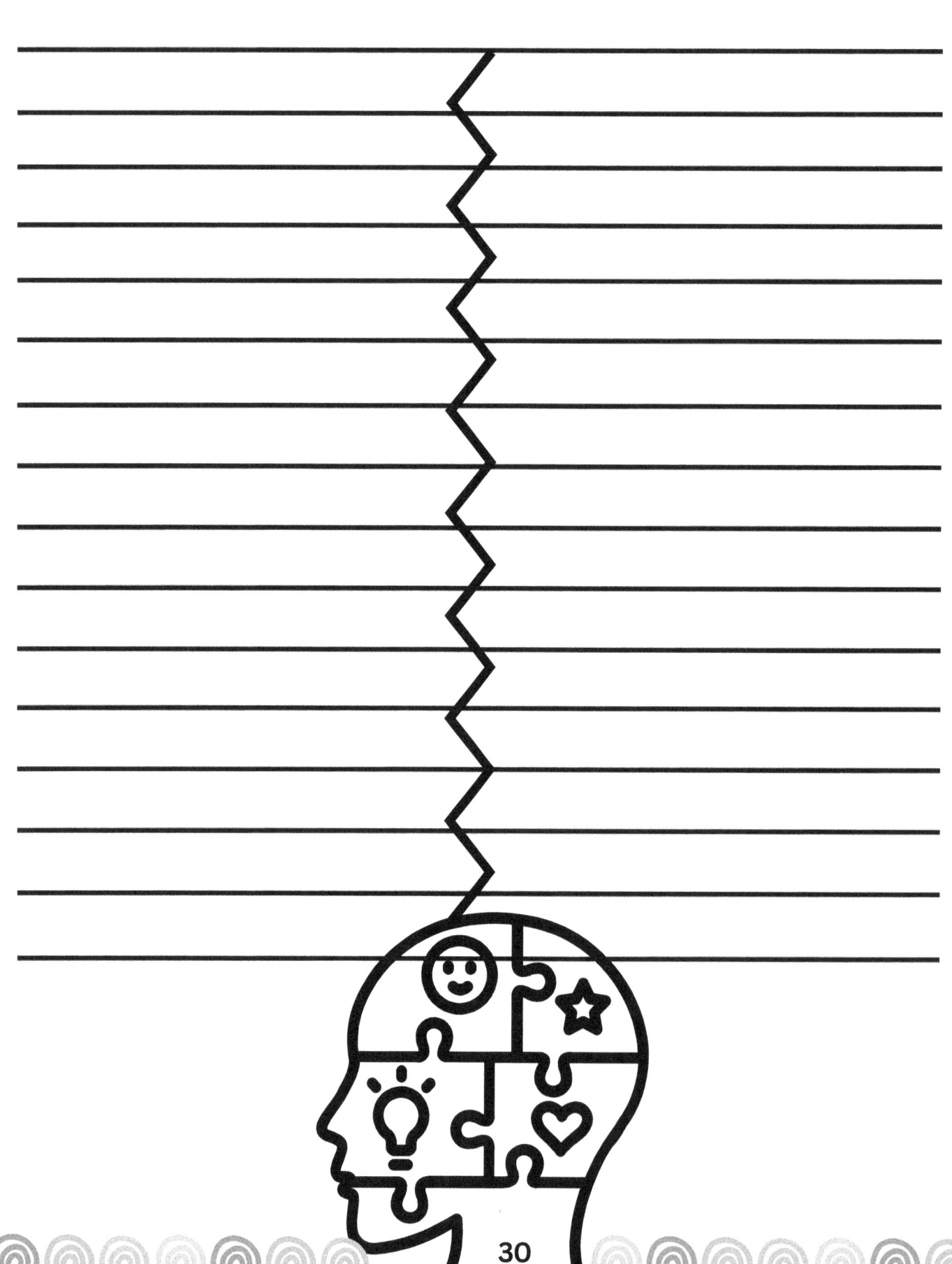

THINGS WE LOVE MOST ABOUT EACH OTHER

_____

_____

_____

_____

_____

_____

_____

_____

_____

_____

_____

_____

_____

_____

"Before We Marry"
Communicator Journal/Keepsake

Part 7
"Money & Finance"

$

HOW WE VIEW AND MANAGE MONEY

Fill in the pie chart together, from most important expense to least important expense. Don't be afraid to color outside the lines.

BUDGETING, SAVING AND FINANCIAL GOALS

_____

_____

_____

_____

_____

_____

_____

_____

_____

_____

Savings

Rent

Bills

List your combined, most
important finances and
how you plan on separating
"needs" from "wants".

Financial Responsibilities and Decision-Making

Full in each block with a financial responsibility. Talk about the importance of them out accordingly

"Before We Marry"

Communicator Journal/Keepsake

Part 8
"Home and Lifestyle"

Where We Want to Live...

Whether you rent or buy, where do you see yourselves planting your permanent roots?

_____

_____

_____

_____

_____

_____

_____

_____

_____

_____

_____

_____

_____

Household Roles and Expectations

Talk about what roles each partner is expected to handle.

_____

_____

_____

_____

_____

_____

_____

_____

_____

_____

_____

_____

_____

_____

_____

_____

_____

Daily Routines and Shared Responsibilities

List some of your daily duties and how you plan to combine and maneuver around them.

○ ....
○ ....
○ ....
○ ....
○ ....
○ ....
○ ....
○ ....
○ ....
○ ....
○ ....
○ ....
○ ....

"Before We Marry"

Communicator Journal/Keepsake

Part 9 "Children & Parenting"

Do We Want Kids?

Why or Why Not?

_____

_____

_____

_____

_____

_____

_____

_____

_____

_____

_____

_____

_____

_____

Parenting Styles and Values

Compare parenting styles in back of book. Discuss which best describes your type of, or parenting styles you want to emulate.

HOW WE PLAN TO BALANCE PARENTHOOD AND MARRIAGE

Talk about how you'll balance being partners and parents. Use this page to share ideas for staying close, making time for each other, and supporting one another through the busy seasons.

_____

_____

_____

_____

_____

_____

_____

_____

_____

_____

_____

_____

_____

faith

love

hope

"Before We Marry"
Communicator Journal/Keepsake

Part 10
"Faith & Beliefs"

Our Personal Beliefs and Values

_____

_____

_____

_____

_____

_____

_____

Hers

Write down what's most important to you—your beliefs, values, and what you care about most. Share and listen to each other with an open mind.

His

_____

_____

_____

_____

_____

_____

_____

How Faith/Spirituality Plays a Role in Our Marriage

Write down what's most important to you—your beliefs, values, and what you care about most. Share and listen to each other with an open mind.

_____

_____

_____

_____

_____

_____

_____

_____

_____

_____

_____

_____

_____

_____

_____

Religious or Cultural Traditions We Want to Follow

Talk about what matters most to each of you- like faith, culture & tradition.

_____

_____

_____

_____

_____

_____

_____

_____

_____

_____

_____

_____

_____

_____

_____

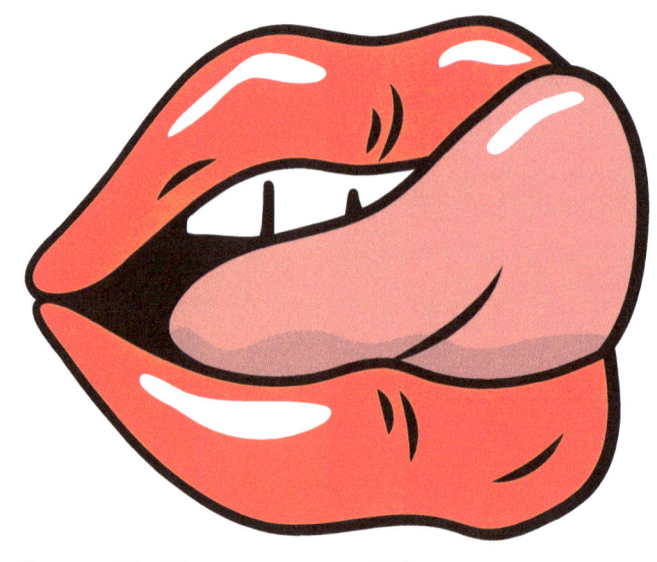

"Before We Marry"
Communicator Journal/Keepsake

Part 11 "Fun & Intimacy"

Ways We Keep the Spark Alive

What are some ways for you and your partner to keep the SPICE in your marriage?

Adventures and Experiences We Want To Share

Adventure is everywhere! Plan a fun and unforgettable experience with your partner.

ADVENTURE

Bucket List for Our Marriage

♡ _____

♡ _____

♡ _____

♡ _____

♡ _____

♡ _____

♡ _____

♡ _____

 Start a bucket list during your engagement. Check them off as you complete them, during your marriage. See how long it takes to complete!

"Before We Marry"

Communicator Journal/Keepsake

Part 12

"Vows & Promises"

Letters to Each Other

❦

Our Vows

Use this space for writing letters to each other

54

I Vow...

_____

_____

_____

_____

_____

_____

_____

_____

_____

_____

_____

_____

_____

_____

We  Do!

I Vow...

Through every page of this journal, we've laughed, reflected, and dreamed together. We've talked about love, challenges, and the future ahead. But at the heart of it all, one simple truth remains: we choose each other.

Marriage isn't just about the big milestones—it's about the everyday ones. The inside jokes, the unexpected adventures, the way we show up for each other in small but meaningful ways. It's about building a life where love isn't just felt but nurtured, celebrated, and strengthened with time.

Before we close this chapter and step into the next, let's take a moment to reflect on our journey together:

- What's something small I do that always makes you smile?
- What's one adventure we haven't taken yet, but can't wait to experience together?
- If we could pick one word to describe our relationship, what would it be? Why?
- What's one way we can keep our love fun and exciting as the years go by?
- What's a dream we both share that we're excited to build together?

Now, let's make a promise to always hold onto the love, laughter, and connection that brought us here. Whether it's a pinky promise, a fist bump, or a kiss—let's seal this with love!

No matter what comes next, always remember:
Love is a choice we make every single day. And today, we choose us!

Appendix

Personality Traits P.19

Positive	Negative
Helpful	Challenging
Uplifting	or Harmful

Career Aspirations

Career aspirations are the goals, dreams, or ambitions someone has for their professional life.

Types of Family Dynamics P.30

Healthy (Supportive & Balanced)

Enmeshed (Overly Involved)

Disengaged (Distant & Isolated)

Chaotic (Unstable & Unpredictable)

Authoritarian (Strict & Controlling)

Permissive (Lenient & Indulgent)

Parenting Styles

Authoritative Balanced

Balance & Suppoortive

Authoritarian Strict & Controlling

Permissive Inumvolvd & Distant

Creative & Analytici

Patient & Ambicious

Empathetic & Logical

Personality Traits that Complement Each Other

 Intraverted & Extroverted

Patent & Amibituous

 Patient & Ambicious

 Empathetic & Logical

 Adventurous & Cautious

 Organized & Flexible

 Organized & Flexible

 Flexible

Resources

- **Conflict Management Styles**
https://courses.lumenlearning.com/wm-organizationalbehavior/chapter/conflict-management-styles/

- **Personality Quiz**
https://www.16personalities.com/free-personality-test

- **Full Love Language Test**
https://5lovelanguages.com/

https://chatgpt.com/

Canva.com

x

Tear here. Place where extra space is needed.

Make sure to check out our entire "Before We" Book series

Before We Move In

Before We Divorce

More books to come...

About The Author

A proud New Jersey native, Adilah Eleam is a passionate wife and creative visionary behind this fun and meaningful communicator journal for couples. Though not a marriage counselor or relationship expert by trade, Adilah brings heartfelt intention, real-life experience, and a deep love for connection into every page she pens.

Motivated by her own journey and a desire to see couples thrive, she created Before We Marry as a lighthearted yet purposeful keepsake to help couples explore the foundation of their relationship before saying "I do." With thoughtful prompts, playful activities, and plenty of space for real talk, her goal is simple: to spark honest conversation, deepen understanding, and help love grow stronger.

This journal isn't about being perfect, it's about being prepared, present, and passionate about building a life together.

Before We Marry

A fun, real-talk journal for couples ready to say "I do"—and mean it.

You've found your person—and now it's time to build something strong, deep, and real.
This journal helps you press pause on the wedding checklist and focus on the connection that matters most: yours.

With a mix of meaningful prompts and playful moments, Before We Marry gives you space to talk, laugh, reflect, and get clear on what forever looks like for both of you.

Inside you'll explore:
💬 How you both handle conflict (and how to do it better)
💰 What money, goals, and shared responsibilities really mean to each of you
👨‍👩‍👦 Family dynamics and how they'll shape your own
🛋️ What everyday life might actually look like after "I do"
💖 How to keep love, fun, and friendship alive through it all

Whether you're newly engaged or just starting the conversation, this journal is your chance to build a strong foundation—and a love story that lasts.

Because a beautiful wedding is great—but a connected marriage is everything.

www.ingramcontent.com/pod-product-compliance
Lightning Source LLC
Chambersburg PA
CBHW041152120626
46547CB00020B/3193